The Garden Club

M.J. Sherman

Copyright © 2019 by M.J. Sherman

All rights reserved.

No part of this book may be reproduced in any form or by any electronic or mechanical means including information storage and retrieval systems, without permission in writing from the publisher.

Printed in the United States of America

First Printing February 2019

ISBN 978-1-68454-154-6 Paperback

Published by: Book Services
www.BookServices.us

Contents

Dedication v

1. Three Girls 1
2. The Old Shed 7
3. A Discovery 15
4. Huggermugger 23
5. A Treasure in the Woodpile 29
6. The Game Begins 35
7. An Astonishing Discovery 53
8. New Holstein, 2090 69

Dedication

To my granddaughter Hannah, who set me in the right direction. And to my husband, Mike, who always encourages me and keeps me on track.

Chapter One
Three Girls

She was twelve and a half. Her hair was a rebellious mop of dishwater blond straw that couldn't be tamed with a comb, a brush, or mousse. Her large eyes appeared to be gray or green, depending on what she wore, although she never noticed because she simply wore whatever she laid her hands on first when she got up in the morning, and she rarely looked in the mirror. She'd rather ride her bike or play baseball than wear a dress and go to a party.

Her name was Gert—short for Gertrude, for heavens sake!—and she was as solidly built as an athlete. She passed most of her time after school alone, investigating the less-inhabited areas of her town and the fields and wooded hills around it. She knew more about her surroundings than anyone else in the area. She had surprised a sleeping fawn, camouflaged in the dappled shade of an old apple tree in an abandoned orchard. She knew where the wild violets hid in a wooded hollow, where the cowslips grew thick around a pond, and where to find the best blackberries.

What friends Gertrude Bohnn had were few and far between. Although she tried to find something good in everyone, she didn't always succeed. However, those who passed her exacting criteria became friends for life.

She came from a broken home and had little, if any, parental guidance. Fortunately, she had a very good sense of right and wrong, and she almost always chose the right one.

Her mother worked two jobs and was just able to keep a roof over their heads and food on the table. Gert was usually on her own from the time she got out of school until eight o'clock in the evening. Her mother woke her up in the morning and then left for work, leaving Gert to fix her own breakfast and get herself off to school.

There were one or two girls she spent some time with at school, but they weren't really friends, just casual acquaintances. Everyone else she mostly ignored. As soon as school was out in June, Gert was out exploring on her bicycle every day, rain or shine.

She never saw her father again after the divorce because he traveled for work so much. For the first few years, she got postcards from the cities where his work sent him. Sometimes they came from overseas,

Chapter 1 - Three Girls

but then they dwindled, and eventually they stopped arriving altogether.

Gert missed the postcards even more than she missed her father; those cards from foreign cities sparked her imagination and her longing to be somewhere, anywhere, other than here in this town, alone. But she steeled herself and never showed that longing and vulnerability to anyone. It would destroy her. She couldn't let anyone see that there was a young girl longing for love and acceptance under this hard outer shell.

~

She was twelve, with curly red hair and freckles. Because her left foot was deformed, she walked with a limp. Her foot could easily have been fixed with surgery when she was born, but there had been no money for the procedure with such a big family, a multitude of boisterous siblings, seven to be precise, plus Mel. She had no actual friends. She had come to the conclusion that that was more than enough people in her life. Her name was Mel. Well, actually it was Melissandra Sanchez, but she only responded to the name Mel.

Mel's family was relatively close. She knew her brothers and sisters loved her, but nevertheless, once in a great while, they teased her about her foot. On the other hand, some classmate or other could be counted on to make fun of her almost every day. She learned early on to just put her head down and power through the day.

The Garden Club

She always hung back when school was over, taking her time to get her books out of her locker and gather up the things she needed to take home with her. She hated the noise and bustle of the students pushing their way out of the building. That was the time they were most likely to notice her and tease her, so she waited until they had cleared out, then walked out a side door and directly to the bike rack.

She pedaled home slowly, stopping occasionally to look at some flowers growing in a flowerbed or to pet a friendly dog or cat. Mel dreaded going home; the commotion her siblings created was as distasteful as the halls when school let out. It was her habit to spend as much time riding around the outskirts of town as she possibly could. Out there in the peace and quiet of the countryside was where she met Gert.

∽

Having just turned 13, Karen Tam was the oldest of the three children in her family and the shyest as well. Although her long, straight hair was actually brown, it was so dark that it often appeared to be black. She wore it pulled back into a braid to keep it out of her eyes and off her face when she rode on her bicycle. Most of the time since they'd moved here, she was outdoors on her bicycle because she was uncomfortable at home.

She had much younger twin siblings, Kenny and Diana. She had been the only child for ten years, and the arrival of the twins had upset her. They were an autonomous unit, and the age difference made it dif-

Chapter 1 - Three Girls

ficult to form any sort of bond with them. They were cute as babies, but they were only interested in each other, and as far as Karen was concerned, she was still an only child who just happened to live in the same house as the twin unit.

As the twins grew past the toddler stage, they had a confidence about them that Karen envied and that made her feel less sure of herself every day. She'd never had a lot of confidence to begin with, and now she had even less. She only managed to just plod along with her head down, taking each day as it arrived.

Karen tried very hard to convince herself to look at things with more self-assurance, but it never seemed to work out. She always felt lacking in some way. So, she spent her time outside on her bike, by herself.

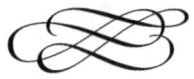

The Garden Club

Chapter Two
The Old Shed

One afternoon, Karen was riding around, exploring her new town, hoping that things would be better here. So far she hadn't seen anything of interest. After half an hour, she decided to turn around and head for home. Continuing on seemed pointless; there didn't appear to be anybody else close to her own age in this whole town. As she turned to start back, she caught movement out of the corner of her eye. She turned her head and saw what appeared to be a young person about her own age rounding the corner and walking towards her. He—or was it a *she*—seemed to be walking with a limp. It looked like the person might have hurt their leg.

She stopped and stood clinging to her bicycle, wondering whether to leave or muster up the courage to talk to whomever it was. *Should I stay and see if this person needs help, or should I just go on past and go home?*

The Garden Club

As the person got closer, Karen saw that it was a girl, stumping along looking down, her curly red hair fluttering in the wind. She was wearing faded jeans, beat-up tennis shoes, and a long, frayed sweater that flapped against her legs.

Karen was torn by indecision. Should she speak to the girl, or should she just ride on? Just as she had decided to pedal on by, the girl looked up and saw Karen standing there holding onto her handlebars like she might fall over if she let go. The girl dropped her gaze and kept on walking. When she came alongside, Karen mustered up her courage and blurted out, "Hi, my name is Karen. What's yours?" The girl stopped, looked at Karen with her sea green eyes and replied, "Mel, my name is Mel. I don't know you."

"No, we just moved here a month ago; you're the first young person I've seen around. Aren't there any other people our age around here?" By this time, Mel had turned and was stumping off past Karen down the sidewalk.

Karen turned and watched her limping away and thought, "*Well that was odd. She just walked away!*" About 100 yards down the sidewalk, Mel stepped onto the grass and, reaching for the wooden fence beside her, she took hold of a group of planks and pushed on them, creating an opening. As she was about to step through, she turned, beckoned to Karen, and said, "Well, are you coming or not?"

Chapter 2 - The Old Shed

Karen looked around, laid her bike down on the grass, and followed Mel through the fence. As she stepped through and stood up, she stopped and stared. In front of her was what could only be called a castle. It was a gigantic stone monstrosity of a house with wide parapets and several huge towers rising above the roof.

"What is this place? I'm not sure I want to do this," Karen thought.

As if she had read Karen's mind, Mel said, "Don't worry about that. It's just old Mr. Magoo's house. That isn't his real name; he just wears big ol' glasses and reminds us of the cartoon character. We aren't going there anyhow. Me and Gert—you'll meet her in a minute—found this cool shed that we're turning into a clubhouse. Come along, The Master awaits us."

Karen snapped out of her reverie and looked quizzically at Mel, "The Master?"

Mel chuckled and urged Karen to follow her. They turned left to face a weathered stone shed. It had a wooden door made of thick planks with wrought iron hinges and handle. There was a small window in the door and a larger one in the wall beside it, but it was so encrusted with dirt that it didn't provide much light.

Mel knocked three times and whistled, then pulled on the hasp. The door inched open, creaking in protest. Mel glanced back at Karen and chuckled again at the expression on her face. "I just call her 'The Master' because she's older than I am, she has a deep, throaty voice, and she's a born leader. Gert, this is Karen, and I think she'll be a great addition to our gang."

Gert looked up, stared at Karen for a moment and said, "Welcome to The Garden Club. We call it that because this is an old gardener's shed. I'm Gertrude, but you can call me Gert." She cackled loudly and continued, "If Mel brought you, you're welcome here." Her voice boomed like a cannon, and if Karen hadn't been looking directly at her, she'd have thought it was a man talking, not a girl her own age.

Karen smiled shyly; the corners of Gert's mouth twitched and her eyes crinkled—her version of a smile.

The girls spent an hour or so getting to know each other. By the time they left for their respective homes, they were comfortable with each other and agreed to meet again the next day, same time, same place.

As the girls rode off in different directions, each one was thinking about the past hour and what had transpired.

For the first time in a long time, Karen was smiling as she pedaled home. At first, just the corners of her mouth turned up, but then the smile turned into a full-blown grin. She had the feeling that she might just have found friends, actual friends. It might take a little while to be sure, but it certainly felt right.

Mel stumped down the sidewalk with a ghost of a smile on her face. That had been the most interesting

Chapter 2 - The Old Shed

hour she had spent with other people in a long time, and even though Gert had a loud voice, she wasn't really a noisy person. Truth be told, that Karen was a very nice person. She hadn't said anything about Mel's foot, and she hadn't stared at it either. It just might be a good thing to get to know this girl better.

Gert stood just outside the door ruminating over the past hour. She and Mel had known each other for almost a month and had become comfortable with one another. They'd met when Mel had discovered Gert's special place.

While walking in a field on the outskirts of town one day, trying to identify the bird she had heard twittering in the hedgerow, Mel had looked up to see where it was, and there, sitting on a rock, almost hidden by the swaying branches of a willow, was Gert. She was staring off across the field when she suddenly felt like she was being watched. She felt the green eyes staring at her before she looked around and saw Mel standing there.

Mel froze and stared when she first saw Gert. She wasn't sure if she was looking at a boy or a girl, but the person didn't look very friendly. She stared for a moment longer and decided it was a girl about the same age as she was. Mel was turning to walk back to the road and her bike when the girl said, "Hi! I've seen you around school, haven't I?" The voice was so deep and raspy that Karen decided she had been mistaken; this was definitely a boy. Mel hesitated a moment and

The Garden Club

then nodded. Gert scootched over, patted the rock beside her, and added, as if an afterthought, "I'm Gert."

That was how the two had begun their friendship. This was a new experience for each of them. Neither of them had ever had a real friend before.

Mel crawled into bed that night with a feeling of lightness, still smiling. Now there were *three* friends. Before she fell asleep she determined to start cleaning up the shed. She would borrow her mother's cleaning supplies and start with that horrible window.

Sweet dreams Mel.

Karen rode home, also feeling a lightness that was completely foreign to her. She was glad that she had met Gert and Mel; she felt contented with their company. But it would be nice to have something to sit on in the shed. *I saw some old stools in the throw-away pile in the garage. We can use them. I'll put them in the wagon and take them with me tomorrow.* She sighed and drifted off to sleep.

'Night, 'night Karen.

Gert walked home, dreading the empty house, but she had all sorts of ideas chasing each other around in her head. There were so many things the three of them could do together, from fixing up the shed to maybe finding places they could explore around town. That would give them a reason to meet every day.

Chapter 2 - The Old Shed

Oh, it was so nice to have someone to do things with! Maybe tomorrow it would be nice to have a snack. She could make some sandwiches and take them along. *Sleep well Gert.*

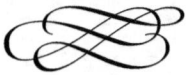

The Garden Club

Chapter Three
A Discovery

The next day, the three girls headed back to their clubhouse feeling much happier than they had in a long time. Each arrived with a sense of excitement bubbling just under the surface.

Mel was the first one to arrive. She had a bucket and cleaning supplies. She was tired of the gloomy interior and vowed to get that window cleaned off *today*.

Karen arrived next, with a wagon hitched to her bike. The wagon contained three stools and some old worn cushions. They were frayed, and they didn't match, but they would be fine for the clubhouse.

Gert arrived in time to help Karen unload the stools and cushions. She turned one stool upside down, set the paper bags she was carrying between the legs of the stool, and put one cushion on top of the bags.

The Garden Club

Karen smiled at Gert and nodded her thanks. They both moved off toward the loose boards and ducked inside.

When the two girls reached the shed, they found Mel hard at work cleaning the dingy window that was the only source of light. Karen and Gert took one look at Mel and burst out laughing.

Mel scowled. "What are you laughing at?"

Karen said, "You've got so many cobwebs in your hair!"

Gert chimed in, "Yeah! It looks like a big spider caught you. Or maybe you're just turning prematurely gray!" Mel felt tears welling up. The only time that anyone laughed at her, it was because of her limp. This laughter was different. It said, *You belong with us.*

The girls spent the rest of their time that day picking up and sweeping. There were mini-mountains of stuff strewn around everywhere. They picked most of it up and bagged it for the trash bin. They found some rough wooden planks and an old wire spool: a cylinder of wood 30 inches across. They rolled and dragged it to the shed to use as a table. When they got it set up in one corner, they all dropped onto the stools, sagging with fatigue. Gert reached into the corner and grabbed the three paper bags she had brought with her earlier. She handed one to Karen, who was sitting closest to her, then leaned forward and gave the second one to Mel. Gert nodded and opened her own bag.

Chapter Three - A Discovery

Peanut butter and jelly had never looked so good! Even the warm soda was wonderful.

After the snack, they fell silent for a few minutes, and then, almost as one voice, they chorused, "Let's explore!"

They found all of the usual gardening items, of course: trowels, rakes, hoes and spades. There were stacks of terra cotta pots of all shapes and sizes, and a number of bags of potting soil, several of which were spilling their contents out onto the floor. There were hose nozzles, garden rakes and leaf rakes, and two dozen of the wire cages that are used to support tomatoes, beans, and flowering vines.

Karen scooted her stool in front of the shelves on the wall by the table. She stood on her tiptoes to see into the top shelf, curious to find out what was up there. "Hey, Gert! Could you hand me that whisk broom that's hanging beside you? I want to clean off these shelves so we can use them for our own things." She dusted energetically, really determined to get rid of the spider webs.

"Do either of you have a flashlight? There's something up here—a box of some sort—but I can't really see it. And I sure don't want to stick my hand in there where I can't see."

Gert and Mel shook their heads.

The Garden Club

"You'll just have to be a brave soldier and reach into the deep, dark depths of that scary place," Gert snickered.

Mel groaned, "Oh, Gert! Can't you just say 'no' and not make a whole speech out of it?"

"No."

The three of them burst into loud guffaws.

Karen laughed so hard she nearly fell off her stool, but nevertheless, she turned and reached timidly into the gloom of the space above her. Her hand closed around a large, flat box. As she pulled it toward the front of the shelf, something fell off the back side of it. She handed the box down to Gert and reached for the item that had fallen onto the shelf.

It was a small, decorative trunk, seven inches long, four inches high, and four-and-a-half inches deep. The designs on the lid looked hand-carved, and it had what looked like black iron hinges and an iron latch.

She handed it to Mel and gingerly raked her hand across the space left by the box and the trunk. Her hand brushed against something flat and round. As she closed her fingers around it, she realized that the round disc was either the base or the top of something. She pulled it towards herself and discovered that it was an hourglass. Amazingly, the thing was intact. She handed it down and stepped off the stool. As she did, Gert reached up and took hold of her hand to steady

Chapter Three - A Discovery

her. Karen hesitated for just a breath of time. "Thank you, Gert. That was very nice. Those stools are a bit rickety." They gathered around the items on the table and began to examine them.

The box, made of cardboard, was in amazingly good condition, which surprised them. In fact, it looked brand new. There was no telling how long it had been sitting up there on that musty, dirty shelf. The writing on it was the only thing that didn't look new; it was oddly faded. All they could make out were the letters "M-U-G-G." Mysteriously, there was almost no dust on the box.

They all reached for the box at the same time. Mel's hand touched it first. She looked at the other two and raised a questioning eyebrow. She waited for a response, and when they both nodded, she lifted the lid.

Inside the box was a gameboard, which she lifted out of the box. Next, she picked up a square of cardboard with a spinner on it. The square was as big as the box. There was a circle on the lower portion of the board, and there were six smaller circles, each with a small hole, arranged in a semicircle around the top of the board. Under the square of cardboard, she found a bag containing five glass disks, each one a different color. The bag also contained five small sharpened pencils and a pad of blank sheets of paper. Under the bag, she saw a second, much smaller, hourglass. This one looked like it would probably measure out a minute of time.

The Garden Club

Finally, there was a small, oblong box. When she lifted the lid, she saw what appeared to be several hundred small cards.

Gert reached over and lifted the lid of the trunk. It also contained cards, but these were colored. Half of them were blue and the other half were red.

They wanted to keep exploring the contents of the box, but it was getting late, and they had to leave. They put it on the middle shelf and pushed it as far back as possible.

Chapter Three - A Discovery

The Garden Club

Chapter Four
Huggermugger

The next day, Karen was the first to arrive at the clubhouse. She wanted to take down the box and look at it some more, but she decided to wait for the other two to arrive. After all, the game belonged to all of them, and it wouldn't be fair for her to look at it all on her own. She left the box on the shelf and distracted herself by doing some more cleaning.

Gert was the next to arrive. She had two old beat-up flashlights and a lantern with her. "See? No more reaching into dark, scary crevices for you, my friend."

Karen nodded, took the flashlights, and put them on the bottom shelf, within easy reach when they were sitting at the table. She set the lantern on the tablecloth she'd brought with her. Gert looked hard at the tablecloth. "Oh, we're being civilized now, are we?"

The Garden Club

Karen looked worried and wondered if she had overstepped the boundary. "I just thought this would keep us from getting splinters from that old wood. It's just an old piece of oilcloth." Gert chuckled and nodded, and Karen visibly relaxed.

Just then, Mel came through the door, carrying what appeared to be either a picnic basket or a soft-sided cooler. Karen cocked her head and raised an eyebrow. "Snacks," Mel announced as she set the basket on the table. "Oooh, nice," she added as she rubbed her hand across the table top. "Look, Ma! No more slivers!"

The three girls dissolved into giggles, then looked embarrassed, and proceeded to get busy straightening things up.

Karen, having waited anxiously for the others to arrive, suggested that they get out the game and try to figure out how it was played. With nods from the other two, Karen jumped up and grabbed the box, the trunk, and the hourglass from the shelf.

As she lifted the lid, a piece of paper the same size as the lid fluttered onto the tabletop. It had a picture of an old fashioned skeleton key on it; under the key was the word "HUGGERMUGGER."

"That's what the faded word on the cover was; all that was left of the word was 'MUGG,' " said Mel. Karen looked up. "You're right, Mel. It's an odd name.

Chapter Four - Huggermugger

I wonder what it means. Why don't one of you look at the paper that fell out and see if it tells us anywhere."

Gert picked up the sheet and started to read it. "Hmm…interesting…I don't see anything." Then she turned it over. "Ah, here it is. HUGGERMUGGER means *in secret*."

They spent the next half hour reading the instructions, hashing out what they didn't understand, and discussing the game in general. The actual gameboard did not say anything about the large hourglass or the blue and red cards in the trunk. They looked in the chest for information, but found nothing there either. Mel picked up the box lid and flipped it over. Taped in one corner was a smaller sheet of paper with the following words written on it:

When a player lands on either a red or a blue key, play stops immediately, and that player draws a card with the corresponding color from the stack in the trunk. Follow the instructions on the card. The large hourglass must be turned over for the adventure to begin, but don't turn it over before you draw and read a card. Enjoy the adventure.

Gert said, "Wow! I wonder what kind of adventure it might be and how we get to it."

Karen and Mel just shook their heads, looking confused and a tiny bit worried.

The Garden Club

Mel looked at the other two and whispered, "These extra pieces don't appear to be part of the original game. It seems to have been altered and the extra parts added to it. Why? And by whom? Why shouldn't the hourglass be turned over before we read the card? What will happen if we do?"

The girls looked at each other. Gert was frowning. Karen looked worried, and Mel was drumming her fingers on the tabletop with an unsettled look on her face.

"I think we should eat our snacks and head home. Gert? Karen? Why don't you put this stuff away while I retrieve our food. We can delve into this again tomorrow if we want. I'm tired, and I can't concentrate right now. What do you say?"

The other two nodded in agreement, and they dug into the basket. They ate in silence, all three of them thinking about the game. After the others had gone, Gert tipped her stool back, put her feet on Karen's vacated stool, and let her mind wander. Half an hour later, she plunked her stool to the floor, stood abruptly, and walked to the door. She glanced back at the box and the trunk resting on the shelf. It kind of spooked her out. She'd have to try to put it out of her mind, or she wouldn't sleep at all tonight.

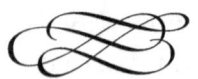

Chapter Four - Huggermugger

The Garden Club

Chapter Five
A Treasure in the Woodpile

The girls arrived at the shed at almost exactly the same time. Mel had just ducked through the fence panels when she heard the brakes squeak on Karen's bike. She waited for Karen to duck through the fence and then fell into step beside her. Just as they reached the door, Gert whistled to them. They waited until she caught up to them, and they all entered the clubhouse together.

The game was sitting on the table where they had left it the night before. They drew their stools together so that they could all see the game, and Mel opened the box.

After an hour's play, Karen said she wanted to go outside and get some air and exercise. They agreed to take a break, and she stepped out the door. As she wandered around the vast estate, she noticed a pile of wood lying off in one corner. Some of it looked kind of interesting from her vantage point. She wandered over to the woodpile and was stunned to see a stack of carved pieces. There were animals and figures, as well as pieces that looked like they could be used as furniture.

She began to rummage through the wood, pulling out and laying aside some pieces that she thought were especially unusual. She had no idea how long she had been digging around in the woodpile, when she heard Mel call to her. As she turned to look in Mel's direction, her eye caught on a large round slab of wood. It looked like an entire slice of tree trunk had been sanded and finished with a thick layer of some sort of glossy finish. She reached into the heap and tried to dislodge the piece. It was heavy as lead. Karen knew that she couldn't move it herself, so she called to Mel, "I'm over here. Come and see what I've found." She showed Mel the carved pieces first. "I thought these would look kind of nice in the clubhouse. We really need to fancy it up a bit, don't you think?"

"Ooh, those are nice. They'll make the place look much better."

"I also found this." Karen pointed to the round slab and looked at Mel. "I think this would make a killer table top."

Mel looked at the wood, then at Karen. "Girl, you have one heck of an eye. That would be ever so much classier than that old sliver-laden thing we made. Let's see if we can get it out of that pile."

Chapter Five - A Treasure in the Woodpile

They tugged and shifted everything around several times, but it was too heavy for them. Mel's bad foot didn't help with the effort. She couldn't maneuver as well as Karen could. Mel stood up, cupped her hands around her mouth, and yelled "Gert, come out here. We need your help! And hurry!"

Gert stuck her tousled head out of the door and shouted back, "This had better be important, or I'll thump the both of you." She ambled across the lawn, stopping occasionally to pick up something on the ground. By the time she reached them, Mel was so antsy that she was practically jumping up and down.

"Look what Karen found. Don't you think this would make a great tabletop? I think it would be much better than what we have now. We tried to get it out, but it's too heavy. We need your help."

"Slow down, Mel. You're going to hyperventilate. Yes, I think it would be wonderful as a tabletop. So let's don't just stand here. Let's get this thing outta here."

The three of them could just barely get the slab up on its edge and roll it across the lawn. Luckily, the way back to the shed was slightly downhill.

When they got to the clubhouse, Mel let go of the slab, hobbled to the door, and propped it open with a stool. She dragged the slabs of wood that made up the old tabletop off the spool and tossed them into a corner. Then she ran back to the door just as Gert and

Karen rolled the round piece through it. It took every ounce of energy and determination to get the new slab up onto wire spool base.

The girls collapsed onto the stools and sighed heavily. They'd done it! They had moved that thing without any help, *and* they had wrestled it onto the base.

Now it was time for a snack and a cool drink of water. Gert reached over to the shelves and pulled the snack bag from where Karen had put it when she arrived. They didn't even care what was in the bags; they just needed something to eat and drink. When they had eaten and rested, they tossed their trash into the half-barrel that they decided would make a great trash can, and as if on cue, they all rose and headed for the door.

"See you tomorrow, Gert, Karen."

"G'bye, Mel. Great effort today. I'm proud of us. See you later," said Gert.

They pedaled slowly home, too tired to hurry, but each with a smile on her face.

Chapter Five - A Treasure in the Woodpile

The Garden Club

Chapter Six
The Game Begins

The next day they all arrived at the same time again, and Gert held the slats while Mel and Karen stepped through. Then she climbed through and followed the other two to the clubhouse.

They played the game several times and were beginning to get the hang of it when Mel spun the dial. She counted her moves and landed on a red key. She looked up at the other two. Gert looked worried but determined, and Karen looked apprehensive, as though she'd rather be somewhere—*anywhere*—else.

They had no idea what to expect, each silently wondering what would happen when Mel turned over the hourglass. She reached across the table and pulled the little trunk to the center of it. She hesitated for just a heartbeat and held out her hand. Karen picked up the hourglass and handed it to her. She slowly lifted the lid of the trunk and picked out the first "time card," as they had decided to call them.

The front of the card said:

LEADVILLE, COLORADO, 1877

On the back of the card were several paragraphs about the chosen destination.

They learned that before it came to be called Leadville, the area had been called Oro City. Gold had been discovered there after the gold rush in California played out. Within a decade, the gold in Oro City was also gone, but the miners discovered silver in the hills and the town name was changed to Leadville. The first gold miners lived in tents on the rough ground below the tree line. When silver was discovered, the town boomed and became a full-fledged city…

Below the information, there was hand-printed lettering. Mel leaned in to see it better and gasped. She froze, clutching the card tightly. Karen reached over and tugged it out of her hand.

It said, *Enjoy the adventure, girls.*

They didn't know whether to cry or run screaming from the shed.

They had sat immobilized for a good ten minutes, saying nothing and doing nothing, when Gert said,

Chapter Six - The Game Begins

"Well, are we just going to sit here, or are we going on an adventure?"

Karen and Mel looked doubtfully at each other; then they looked at Gert. She had a ghost of a smile on her face and a twinkle in her eye. "Let's go for it, girls. What have we got to lose?"

"Our lives?"

"Everything?"

Gert just shook her head and nodded at the hourglass. Mel picked it up, and Gert said suddenly, "Maybe we should hold hands or something." So they did.

They reached across the table and grasped each other's hands. Karen took hold of Mel's right arm; Mel's right hand was holding the hourglass.

"On the count of three. One, two…three."

Gert said, "Well, *that* was anti-climactic. Nothing happened. Let's just call it a day and head home. Maybe tomorrow we'll figure it out."

The other two nodded wearily, and they all headed for the door.

Gert stepped out first and stopped dead in her tracks, so suddenly that Mel and Karen ran into her, knocking her off balance.

The Garden Club

"Why'd you do that, Gert? I thought we were going home," exclaimed Karen. "Yeah, Gert, let Karen and me out!" said Mel.

"Look around, girls," Gert said, her voice an awed whisper. We're not at home anymore. Look over there. Those buildings aren't anything I've ever seen before. Have you?"

Karen and Mel shook their heads, and pushed Gert out so that they could see too. Their eyes followed Gert's gaze. She was looking off to the right, down a dusty, rutted street.

"Where are we? Karen? Gert? Somebody, please talk to me. I'm scared!" Mel was starting to shake, and she reached out and touched the other two. They nodded and reached for each other's hands.

This was not the yard outside the clubhouse! They were standing in a deeply-rutted dirt road facing some tall wooden buildings that appeared to have been constructed in the not-so-distant past because the lumber looked new and not weathered. Huge piles of black dirt were heaped around the base of one of the buildings. What looked like a black and sooty conveyer belt ran from the top of the building to the ground. As they stood there trying to figure out what they were looking at, Gert squeezed the girls' hands. They glanced over at her, and she nodded to their right. An elderly man was shuffling towards them, mumbling to himself as he ambled along.

Chapter Six - The Game Begins

Gert dropped the girls' hands and started towards him. Karen and Mel quickly fell in step beside her, as Mel whispered, "Gert, what are you doing?"

"I'm going to ask this gentleman where the heck we are." Which is exactly what she did.

"Excuse me, sir. My name is Gert, and I would like to ask you a question if I may."

The man, who needed a shave, squinted at her for a time and then nodded his head. "Sure. You may ask me a question; I don't promise I'll answer it, but ask away."

"Can you tell me where we are? My friends and I are on an adventure, and we aren't sure where we ended up."

"An adventure, eh? What sort of adventure would you be on?"

"We are on a trip with our parents and didn't see a sign when we came into town."

The man stood staring off at something, or nothing, or perhaps he was just puzzled. He shook his head and almost fell over. Gert reached out and grabbed his arm as he leaned precariously to the right. He nodded at her and smiled a toothless grin.

"There. Are you steady now? How about if we sit here on this boulder?" She turned him slowly so that

The Garden Club

his back was to the rock. Karen ducked around them and laid her flannel shirt, bunched up, onto the rock, as Gert lowered him slowly onto it. Gert then repeated her explanation and question.

He tilted his head up at her and said in a creaky voice, "Why, thankee, missy, and to answer your question, you're in Leadville, Colorady."

Mel leaned down and said, "Hi, I'm Mel, and this is going to sound strange, but what year is it?"

He squinted at her and murmured, "Pretty young things." Then he replied, "It be 18 and 77."

"Thank you— I'm sorry, but I don't know how to address you."

"Muh name is Charlie, but everyone just calls me Pops."

"Well, thank you, Pops. I know that sounded weird, but I wanted to be sure that everything on our school report was correct." They continued chatting with Pops for a while, getting information about how the town came to be, how long it had been there, and anything else that they thought they could use for a report for their history or geography class.

"Can you tell us how this place came to be called Leadville?" asked Gert.

Chapter Six - The Game Begins

"Yep, sure can. You two, step over here so's you can hear too," he said, motioning to Mel and Karen. "Well, after the Californy gold rush played out, the miners began heading back east. Some went all the way back home. Others continued to prospect as they moved along. Many of 'em hoped to strike it rich here in Colorady, but the ore played out here too. In 1861 there was about 400 mines dotting the area and for a while they yielded lots of ounces. By 1866 a total of about 8000 prospectors had settled in this here area and a sort of city sprung up. They called it Oro City—that means Gold City. But as the placer mines began to play out, Oro City began to decline."

"So what happened to Oro City?" Mel asked. "Is it still there?"

"Well now, young lady, as a matter of fact there are still some buildings there, but the folks has all moved out.

"Most of the miners left here, just like they did in Californy, but some hard-headed fellers thought to keep on a-lookin'. Some kept working the underground mines that were begun by others. About eleven years later, let me see, that'd be about 1861 or so, they noticed that some of the sand they was haulin' out of the mines was partially black . Well, some smart fellas decided to have the black sand assayed—that's just a fancy word for tested for weight or quality—to determine the presence of other minerals."

The Garden Club

Charlie stopped talking to clear his throat, his normally raspy voice starting to sound hoarse.

Mel reached into the pocket of her sweatshirt and pulled out a travel mug, which she carried with her everywhere. She handed it to Charlie. He squinted at it and hesitated before taking it from her. "It's a canteen," she explained. There's cool water in it; please drink a little. It will ease your throat."

"Haint never seen a canteen like this afore, but a wee sip of water might taste good 'bout now."

He drank most of the contents of the bottle. "Thankee, missy. That hit the spot, though I usually drink stuff that's a bit harder than that." He winked at her and handed back the mug. "Now, back to my story. After the gold played out, the miners started moving east again, and some of 'em found some silver in the black dirt that was gettin' into ever'thing. They figgered maybe there was more to be found. So they started digging in the black stuff and realized that this was much easier than mining the gold had been; all they had to do was separate the silver from the dirt. Turns out there was lots of silver here, so they built a new and better city on this spot and named it Leadville, 'cause the black stuff they were shovelin' contained cerussite, which is a lead mineral with a high silver content. The dirt could be processed and the silver removed from it. I'm a thinkin' that there was enough silver found to make 'em all rich."[1]

---

[1] It is said that a total of 82 million dollar's worth of lead was eventually dug out of the Leadville mines.

Chapter Six - The Game Begins

"Wow, Pops! You sure know a lot about this place. How do you know so much?"

Pops chuckled. "Well now, Mel—it is Mel isn't it?—funny name for such a pretty young girl. I know so much 'cause I came here from the Missouri Territory in 18 and 59, a couple of years before Coloradee was even a U.S. Territory. Now, I think I'd best be on my way. Huh, ain't talked so much in many a year. It's been a pleasure, ladies."

Gert and Karen helped Pops up and turned him in the direction he had been going. He patted their hands, nodded his head, and tottered off down the road.

The girls watched for a moment or two, thinking about Charlie and all of the information they had gotten from him. It was all very interesting, but what good would it do them? Each wondered to herself what they had accomplished by coming on this adventure. It's great to know about things that happened in the past, but this didn't seem to have any personal significance for them, other than helping with a school report.

Mel broke the silence by suggesting that they explore Leadville. They had no idea how long they'd be here, so they should probably make the best of the time they had.

As they turned in the opposite direction away from Charlie, they heard a deep rumbling and and felt the earth vibrate under their feet. They saw nothing at first, then Mel saw the wagon heading towards them. "Wow! That wagon is really moving fast. Those horses are at a dead run. That's really dangerous on this rough road!"

"*Look out!*" hollered Karen at the top of her voice.

They jumped out of the way just as the horses came past at a full, out-of-control gallop. They stood shaking in the bar ditch[1] beside the road, looking at the dust cloud curling up behind the wagon.

Karen suddenly screamed, "*Oh No!! Charlieeee!!*' The other two froze momentarily. Then they all sprinted back down the road towards Charlie, or at least to where he had been a few moments ago. Karen got to the rumpled heap that was Charlie first. "Is he dead?" The voice was unidentifiable. It could have been either Mel or Gert asking.

"I don't know. I'm afraid to move him, but I need to see if he has a pulse or even a heartbeat, or *something!*" Karen replied. She looked up and noticed Gert standing back from them. She was pale and shaking. "Gert! Snap out of it! Go find some help—*now!!*" After a second or two, Gert shook her head, looked at the lump of clothing on the road, and sprinted across the grass, heading toward the nearest building. As she ran towards it, she saw that it was the sheriff's office. She dashed up the steps and burst through the door.

---

[1] A borrow ditch or bar ditch is a roadside drainage ditch formed when dirt from the ditch was borrowed to form the crown of the road.

Chapter Six - The Game Begins

Two men were sitting at a huge wooden desk. Behind the desk was an older man with gray hair and a scruffy beard. He was leaning back in his chair with his feet propped up on the edge of the desk, a well-used pipe clenched between his teeth. He had holes in the soles of his boots, though Gert only got a glimpse of the boots because his feet hit the floor as she burst into the room.

The younger man wore dressier clothes: new blue jeans, a vest, and polished boots that looked fairly new. He had shaggy, slightly curly, short blond hair. He had the stump of a cigar in his mouth and was leaning forward, as if the older man was saying something very interesting. Gert stopped in midstep. The younger man looked so familiar, but he couldn't be; she was back in 1877, and she had never been here before. She shook her head to clear it and said breathlessly, "Hurry! There's been an accident. You've got to get the doctor. Charlie's been hurt!" She could barely get the words out, as she was still trying to catch her breath after the sprint across the hill.

"Whoa there, young lady. Slow down and start again. You say somebody is hurt. What happened? Who's hurt?" the sheriff asked.

"Hurry, please! It's Charlie—Pops—he's been hit by a wagon. The horses were galloping really fast, and they just ran right over him and didn't stop! Please find the doctor and help him. I'm afraid he's going to die!" Much to her embarrassment, tears sprang to her eyes. She turned away from the sheriff so he wouldn't

The Garden Club

see her crying. Just then, the younger man brushed past her and sprinted off down the street.

The sheriff put his hands on Gert's shoulders and pushed her down onto the chair that the younger man had just vacated. "Erick has gone to get the doctor. You can relax now. Here, drink this." The sheriff handed her a glass with a tiny bit of amber liquid in it. Gert swallowed the liquid in one gulp. She sputtered and then coughed. She gave the sheriff such a stunned look that he chuckled. "What was that? That was awful! Are you trying to kill me?" she gasped.

"Sorry, young lady, but you were getting so excited, I was afraid you were going to faint. I didn't want to take the time to go for water, and it was the only thing at hand. It was the last of my morning glass of whiskey."

"*Whiskey*? You gave me whiskey? And I don't faint! Some silly women might faint when they get excited, *BUT—I—DON'T!!*

"Okay, okay, Gert—you did say that was your name, didn't you? How about you start at the beginning and tell me what happened."

"All right, but I'm not sitting here any longer. I've got to get back to my friends and find out how Pops is doing." *If he's alive*, she mumbled under her breath.

"All right, let's go." He reached out to help her out of the chair, but when he saw the look in her eyes,

Chapter Six - The Game Begins

he chuckled softly and strode to the door. He pulled it open and motioned for her to precede him. Gert stood, and with all the dignity she could muster, marched past him into the street, retracing her steps to the scene of the accident. The sheriff, still chuckling softly, fell into step beside her.

When they arrived, the doctor was just rising from his examination of Charlie. He nodded his head in response to something Charlie said and turned to say something to Mel and Karen. Gert saw them talking to the younger blond-headed man. She dashed over to them, and in her usual not-so-subtle way, demanded, "Well, what'd Doc say? Will Charlie be all right? Do they have any idea who did this? *Does anybody know anything?*"

Mel reached out, put her hand on Gert's arm, and quietly replied, "The doctor thinks Charlie will survive. He's a tough old guy, and it's only a broken leg and some bruises. It looks like he got knocked down, but not trampled by the horses. It appears that the broken leg was caused by a wagon wheel running over it. He'll be okay."

"Well, he'd better be," Gert replied, "or I'll—I'll—oh heck, I don't know what I'll do!"

The young man was madly writing in his notebook. He glanced up when the girls stopped talking, and said to Gert, "Hi, I'm Erick Bohnner, a reporter for *The Reveille*. It's the first newspaper to be printed in Leadville. Your friends here have been filling me in

The Garden Club

on what happened Would you care to add anything to the story?"

"Yeah," Gert snarled, "Find that so-and-so and throw him in jail. He could have killed our friend here. He ran Pops down and didn't even bother to stop or come back to see if he was hurt or even alive!" Under her breath she added, *the scumbag!*

Erick must have heard her, because he stopped writing and glanced up at Gert. He stared at her for just a moment, shook his head, and continued writing. He turned to Karen and Mel and said, "Okay, ladies. I guess that's all for now. I hope your friend is okay. He nodded to them and turned back to Gert. He gave her one last, long look and headed back to his office.

There was something about Gert that he couldn't put his finger on. She seemed familiar, in a way, but he knew he hadn't met her before. Oh well, he'd figure it out eventually. After all, that's what reporters did: they figured things out and wrote about them.

The girls returned with the sheriff to his office. He asked them to recount the incident, since he'd only gotten part of the story from Gert and needed to fill in the details if he was going to find the person who did this. As they told their story again, the sheriff occasionally interrupted to ask a question. "Yes," Karen said, "the horses were a matched pair of grays with colorful, decorative halters. And the wagon was quite large. Not something one took out for a ride around

Chapter Six - The Game Begins

town. It was more of a lumber wagon size. It looked like it would be used for hauling big loads of stuff."

The sheriff nodded. He leaned his chair back, propped his feet on the desk, and picked up the pipe, which he clamped between his teeth. He looked up at the three of them. They all had questioning looks on their faces. He chuckled, pulled the pipe from his mouth, and said, "It helps me think. I rarely actually smoke this. Besides, it gives me the appearance of being deep in thought. That seems to be important to most people, and as a bonus they are less likely to interrupt me." The girls relaxed a bit and smiled as they said goodbye and started out the door. As Mel, the last in line, was stepping through the door, the sheriff called out, "Where can I find you if I have more questions?" And then realized he was talking to the door. He got up, strode across the room, and pulled the door open to repeat his question, but all he saw was a shimmer in the air above the road where the accident had happened.

Erick stepped out of the newspaper office, ready to dig up more news for the paper. He looked toward the sheriff's office just as the girls disappeared over the rise that separated the town from the road. He saw a glimmer in the air over the spot where the accident had happened. He stood for a moment, wondering about Gert. Why did he have the feeling that he knew, or at least recognized, her? Well, that line of thought would have to wait until another day. He had stories to dig up.

The Garden Club

The girls glanced back as they got to the road where Charlie had been injured. They observed a slight shimmering in the air around them and felt a gentle breeze kiss their faces. And the next thing they knew, they were in the yard in front of the clubhouse.

Mel and Karen stood outside the door, thinking about the events they had just experienced, the strange encounter with Charlie, and the accident. It didn't seem real, and yet they had been there, involved in all of it.

Gert was thinking about the adventure too, but her mind kept going back to Erick. She was sure she knew him somehow, but until today she had never even seen him in her imagination. She kept seeing that mop of blond curly hair, so much like hers, the way he shook his head when he was thinking, and the twist of his mouth when he talked. It was as if she had seen it before. Oh well, that's for another time, right now they had to get inside and decompress. Boy, this time-adventure thing was tiring.

They all gasped, and Mel whispered, "Did that really just happen? Are we really back here? This wasn't a dream, was it?"

Karen turned to Mel and replied "Oh, we're back! Were we *really* in Leadville, or did we just imagine that?"

Gert's reply was a sudden dash into the clubhouse, with the other two close behind. She was staring at

Chapter Six - The Game Begins

the hourglass when they came through the door. "I think we've only been gone for an hour. See? Most of the sand is in the bottom, and when time ran out, we came back."

They simultaneously plopped down on the stools, and each sighed and dropped her head onto the table. They didn't know whether to laugh or cry or get out of the shed as fast as possible. But whichever they did, should they destroy the game first? The trip through time had been scary, but they were all fascinated by what had just happened.

They had risen from the stools and headed for the door before any of them realized they had even moved.

"See you later, Gert."

"Yeah, 'bye Mel, Karen."

They walked to their bikes in silence, and each headed for home.

The Garden Club

Chapter Seven
An Astonishing Discovery

The girls had been back at school for almost a month when they played the game again. This time it was Karen who landed on a key—a blue one. Blue indicated the future.

When Karen pulled the card from the trunk she was confused. The card gave them a date, 2090, but not a place. They considered the lack of information on the card and decided that they should postpone the adventure until the weekend.

Karen wondered whether they should just postpone it entirely. Gert grabbed the instruction sheet from the box, spread it out on the table, and began to peruse it. "Nowhere does it say that we have to go on the adventure immediately. It doesn't say that we have to do it now, but it also doesn't say we can't wait until later."

The Garden Club

Karen and Mel nodded. "Mel and I think we should wait until the weekend. That way, if it does take more than the hour indicated by the hourglass, we won't miss school, though I don't know if that's such a bad thing after all. Do you agree, Gert, or do we take a vote on it?"

"Well, Karen, I guess I'll agree, because, obviously, I wouldn't win in a vote. Besides, I think it's a smart idea."

"Okay then," said Mel. "We'll meet here Saturday morning and see if this will work. Be careful when you move the hourglass, we don't want you to inadvertently wind up in the future without us." Karen nodded and gingerly lifted the hourglass to the shelf, then put the game box on the shelf above it. As this was already Thursday, the three girls exited the shed and headed home. They would have to get up for school in the morning, and they all had homework to do.

In the late 1950s and early 1960s, many small schools combined several grades in one class. If there were only three or four students from one grade, the school would have the students in a lower or higher grade take the same class. This meant that the teacher didn't have to teach the class several semesters in a row. It also explains why Karen had a history class with Mel and Gert and why it turned out to be the perfect assignment for them.

In history class the next day, they were given an assignment that really excited them. Mr. Graves told

Chapter 7 - An Astonishing Discovery

the fifteen students that they would be doing a project in groups of three. They were to pick a time and a place in the past and find as much information about it as they could. The three students in each group would all receive the same grade on the project.

Immediately, three hands went up and three voices called out. Mr. Graves looked at the three girls in surprise. These three were usually the quiet ones, the ones who never drew attention to themselves, and here they were, calling to get his attention. Good. Maybe they're coming out of their shells.

"Yes, Karen, you may go first."

"Gert, Mel, and I would like to work together. We know what we want to do."

"All right, Mel, you're next. Where and when?"

"We'll do Leadville , Colorado."

"Gert, what year do you want to do?"

"We're choosing the late 1800s.

"All right. Leadville, Colorado, late 1800s, is off the list."

The girls were excited, because they had gotten quite a lot of information from Charlie. They only needed to add a bit more, and they would have a great report, which would surely get them an A.

~

When Karen arrived at the clubhouse on Saturday, Gert was sitting on her stool with an encyclopedia on the table in front of her.

"Gert! You're here early— Wow! What have you got there? Where'd you get that? Is the library open this early on Saturday?"

"If you must know, I brought it from home, along with those over there." She pointed to the shelves. "My father bought them for me the year before he left us. Where's Mel? Why isn't she here yet? I don't want to have to go over all of this a second time."

"Well, hello to you too, Gert. What's the encyclopedia for? Hello Karen." Gert and Karen looked at Mel and nodded. "What's going on here? Did I say or do something wrong? Gert, why are you scowling?"

"Mel, why are you so confused? Gert *always* scowls," Karen teased. "Actually, we were just waiting for you to get here. Gert has some more info on Leadville that she wanted to share with us, and she doesn't want to have to go over it twice. You know how impatient she is."

"Yeah, I know."

Chapter 7 - An Astonishing Discovery

Gert's scowl deepened. "Do you want to hear this, or should we all just go for an F on our report?"

"I'm sorry, Gert. Go ahead. I've got my notebook here. I'm ready when you are." Gert looked at the other two and cleared her throat. Mel and Karen rolled their eyes at each other, then turned their attention to Gert. She began reading about Leadville. It was pretty much what Charlie had told them. But they found enough additional material to expand what they already knew into a well-written report.

They decided to postpone their next adventure until they had handed in the report and gotten the A they expected from Mr. Graves.

∽

It had been two weeks since the girls had turned in their report. Their growing curiosity had made them eager to get on with their next adventure, but they were on edge about Mr. Graves' reaction to their project. They all felt an uneasiness that they couldn't account for. Gert was sure that the information they had gotten directly from Charlie had added authenticity and enough interesting detail to warrant a top grade.

Waiting was so hard. They were in the clubhouse on a beautiful Saturday morning with a light breeze and puffy white clouds sailing along in a powder blue sky. They should have been feeling relaxed and happy. That was not the case. For the first time, they couldn't

The Garden Club

think of anything to do. They had cleaned every nook and cranny, the windows were sparkling, and they had pulled up the long grass around the front step. Mel finally suggested that they go out and explore the property. After all, that's how she had found the cool wood carvings and the tabletop. Maybe they could find more neat stuff. If nothing else, it would kill some time. After about an hour, having turned up nothing of interest, they gathered up their back packs, got on their bikes and pedaled slowly home.

At the end of history class the following Monday, Mr. Graves asked Gert, Mel and Karen to remain in their seats . They looked at each other and worried. Mr. Graves didn't keep students after class to praise them for their good work; he did that in front of the whole class. This didn't look good. What could they possibly have done wrong? They knew that the information from Charlie was accurate, so what could it be?

Mr. Graves came over and sat down at one of the desks. "Girls, I'm sorry to have to tell you this, because your report is probably the best one out of the whole lot. I'm afraid I'm going to have to give you a zero on your report. The last part, where you mention the old gentleman's giving the information about his accident to the reporter, cannot be corroborated. I've looked into several historical documents, and there is no mention of this event in any of them. I'm sorry, but that part throws your whole report into question. I will give you until next class period to either admit you just added that part for effect, or to somehow come up

Chapter 7 - An Astonishing Discovery

with proof that it actually happened. I will give you the grade the report deserves. It's up to you."

The three of them sat, stunned. They had no idea what to do. They couldn't tell Mr. Graves that they wrote about Charlie's accident because they had actually witnessed it. That would sound even crazier than the actual mention of the accident.

Unfortunately, they either had to take the zero and stick to their guns or remove the part that authenticated it. What else could they do? They rose from their desks, walked solemnly to their bikes, and pedaled slowly to the clubhouse.

They sat around the table lost in thought. Someone had to find a solution, or they were all in trouble. Mel was the first to stand. She stretched, scratched her leg and said, "Well, girls, that was quite an adventure, but we'll never be able to prove any of it, so I guess we'll just have to eliminate the best part and take a mediocre grade on a mediocre report. *Or* we can leave it, take the zero, and I'll just have to tell my parents that I messed up. This was going to be my chance to prove to them that I really *am* the kind of student they want me to be. I'll see you all tomorrow if I'm not grounded for the rest of my life." And with that, she turned and limped out the door, heading for home, her whole demeanor radiating defeat.

As Karen and Gert watched her walk out the door, they felt exactly like Mel looked. Gert shook her head. "Wow, I haven't seen her look like that since the day I met her. We've just *got* to do something! I can't stand to see her like this. She used to be super self-conscious about her foot, but since we've gotten together she's really come out of her shell. Karen, we've got to do something. I'm really worried about her."

"I am too, Gert. I'll try to think of something. Let's see if, between the two of us, we can find a solution. Okay?"

Gert nodded and waved as Karen headed out the door. An hour later, Gert also pedaled home. When she got there, she headed straight to her mother's room. She paused momentarily at the door, then entered and went straight to the closet.

She remembered that just after her father left, she had sat on the bed in this room asking questions about her father while her mother was brushing her hair and getting ready for work. She remembered jumping off the bed and wandering around the room, looking at things her mother had sitting out. There was a box. It looked like a shoe box, but much bigger than the one her new shoes came in. It was probably big enough to hold her daddy's shoes. She asked her mother about it, and her mother replied, "Don't worry about that. It's some stuff your father left here when he moved on. I'll probably just toss it out."

After her mother left for work that day, Gert had gone back to the bedroom and found the box on a pile of stuff that was going to the trash. She took the box off the pile and shoved it into the far back corner of

Chapter 7 - An Astonishing Discovery

the closet. She sometimes thought about that box, but just never felt the need to look into it. Until now. Now, for some reason, she felt a strange urgency to find out what was in that box. Hopefully, her mother hadn't found it and tossed it out.

She reached into the corner. There it was! Still there after all these years. Why hadn't her mother thrown it out? As she stood there holding it, her mind was spinning. Why was she holding this box? What could it possibly contain that would do her any good? And why would she want anything that he had left behind? Maybe it would be like opening Pandora's box and finding out things that she didn't want to know.

She finally shook herself out of her reverie and carried the box to her room. She set it on her desk. Then she sat on her bed and stared at it. As she sat there looking at the box, a voice in her head told her to get off her butt and open the darned thing. She had a feeling that it was important, and that she needed to do this now before she lost her nerve.

She got off the bed, sat down at the desk, and picked up the box. She held it a moment before she finally lifted the lid. The first thing that met her eyes was an old photograph of her grandparents. She was stunned to see that her grandfather had blue eyes and curly blond hair just like hers. Gert had never met her grandfather; he had died before she was born. She turned the photograph over and read the names neatly hand-printed on the back: Johann Eric Bohnn and Elizabeth Gertrude Bohnn. The photograph was dated 1901. Gert felt dizzy and disoriented. She nearly fainted. She was named after her grandmother, and her grandfather's middle name was Eric!

Her father's name was John E. Bohnn! Bohnner was close enough to Bohnn to be a match! The reporter whom she had talked to in Leadville could be a relative. That may have been why he seemed so familiar to her. She propped the photo up on the desk and stared at it for several minutes. She could see the resemblance between her grandfather and Erick Bohnner, as well as an uncanny similarity between Erick and her father.

Gert began pulling things out of the box: postcards, obituaries, more old photos. She glanced briefly at each item, then reached for the next one. At the very bottom was one last item: a newspaper clipping, yellowed with age and torn around the edges, with a smudge or two here and there. There was a piece of notepaper clipped to the edge of the article. Gert carefully unclipped the note and unfolded it. The handwriting was familiar; it was identical to the writing on the post cards she had gotten from her father when he was traveling.

The notepaper had just two words on it: *Grandpa Erick?* Gert sat in her desk chair, holding tightly to the photo, tears running down her cheeks. She picked up the clipping and with trembling hands and blurry eyes, she read the article. It was the one that Erick had written on the day that Charlie had been run over. The name of the newspaper was absent but the date

Chapter 7 - An Astonishing Discovery

was visible in the byline—Erick J. Bohnner Friday, June 15, 1877, Leadville.

By this time Gert was trembling so hard that she couldn't hold onto the article. It fluttered to the desktop and stared back at her.

She *had* to show this to Karen, and most of all, to Mel! She really hated calling people. They always expected some polite conversation before getting the person to whom the call was placed, but this was important!

She dialed Karen's number first, "Hi, Karen, it's Gert. You need to meet me at the clubhouse *now*. It's extremely important! Just tell your parents that you're coming over here to study for a test. Don't ask questions, just do it! She immediately hung up and dialed Mel's number. As she expected, she got one of Mel's siblings, and it took forever for Mel to pick up. When she finally heard Mel say hello, Gert repeated the message, adding the part about studying at her house. "Hurry! It's important!" she practically shouted into the phone.

Gert hung up the phone, grabbed her jacket, picked up the photo and the article, and dashed out to her bike. As she rounded the corner by the clubhouse, she saw Karen jump off her bike and head for the fence slats. She whistled and pedaled to where Karen had dropped her bike. Gert dropped hers beside Karen's. Karen immediately started asking questions. "Wait till Mel gets here. I don't want to have to go through this twice. I hope she gets here soon. I can hardly wait to show you what I found."

"Here's Mel now," Karen said. "Let's get to the clubhouse fast. I think I'm more anxious than you are, Gert!"

"Hurry up, Mel," both girls cried at once. Mel jumped off her bike, and they all stood and watch as it continued rolling onto the grass before coming to rest beside the other two on the grass. Despite the stress and anxiousness of the situation, they all laughed at the sight of the bike coming to rest beside its friends. "Wow, Mel, nice dismount!" Karen chuckled as they all crawled through the slats and ran to the shed.

Gert grabbed the lantern because it was much dimmer inside the shed than outside. She banged it down on the table and flipped it on. She motioned the other two to sit. They laughed and followed The Master's orders. Gert cleared her throat and pulled out the photo and the article. She held them up and exclaimed, "Voila, I have here the means of our salvation!"

Mel and Karen rolled their eyes. Karen said, "Enough with the dramatics, Gert. Why did we have to get here so quickly? My parents were curious about my suddenly having to study for a test."

"Yeah, mine were too," Mel echoed. "Couldn't this have waited until tomorrow?"

Chapter 7 - An Astonishing Discovery

"No! This is extremely important!"

"So tell us already," Mel replied.

Gert slowly placed the photo and the article on the table, sat back and waited. Mel reached over and picked up the photo. "Who is this, and what does it have to do with why we're here?"

"That, my dear, is a photograph of my grandparents."

"What does this have to do with our hurrying over here?" Mel looked peeved. "You got us down here just to show us an old photo?"

Ignoring her questions, Gert said, "Now look at the newspaper clipping and read the note attached to it."

Karen leaned forward and read aloud as Mel flipped the photo to the back side. "Grandpa Johann Eric? Who the heck is Grandpa Johann Eric, and what does this have to do with why we're here? C'mon, Gert. What's this all about anyhow?" She looked annoyed. Karen, too, was not very happy.

"That was all it said. But what's important is that it was written by my father."

"So?" the other two asked in unison. "That still doesn't tell us the relationship between the photo and this old newspaper clipping. Which, by the way, is about to fall apart."

Gert looked at the other two and said "Look closely at the photograph. Does the man look familiar?"

"Well, he looks a little bit like you," Mel replied. "And he looks a lot like—Oh, what was the name of that reporter in Leadville?" She wrinkled her brow in thought for a minute. "Hey! Wasn't it Erick something?"

"Yes it was," said Karen. "his name was Erick Bhonner! But I still don't get the connection." Gert's reply stunned them both. "My father's name is John E. Bohnn II. Now , look at this article."

Karen jumped up, tipping her stool over as she did so. "I've got it! That reporter was your great grandfather! Erick J. Bohnner was the father of your grandfather, whose name was...?"

"Johann E. Bhonn," Gert answered.

"So," Mel added, "Erick Bhonner was your great grandfather? No wonder he looked so familiar to all of us. Wow!"

"Now, to answer your question, 'What does this have to do with why we're here now,' read the whole article, Mel."

Longtime resident injured in accident today. Run over by out-of-control wagon read the lead line. "That's the proof we need to get an "A" on our report. I don't have to give Mr. Graves the information about the

Chapter 7 - An Astonishing Discovery

family connection. We just need to prove that the accident actually happened, and there it is." Gert had tears in her eyes as she finished her statement. She saw that the other two did as well. She gave them her fiercest scowl and then chuckled, "Okay, I'm tearing up over this, and so are the two of you. It's no big deal."

"Yay! Gert saves the day!" Mel and Karen shouted. Mel laughed and said, "Now I don't have to explain why I got such a lousy grade on the history report, and I won't be grounded for the rest of my life!"

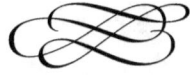

The Garden Club

Chapter Eight
New Holstein, 2090

Gert showed Mr. Graves the old newspaper article when she turned in the report. On Friday, Mr. Graves returned the reports. At the top of their report, in red, was a big, fat A-plus! Their parents were so thrilled that they got together and planned a Saturday night event at Karen's house.

The girls gathered at the clubhouse on Saturday morning. It was a beautiful autumn Saturday. The sugar maples embracing the clubhouse had turned bright orange, yellow, and red, and the smell of woodsmoke was in the air. Tonight they would be roasting hot dogs and marshmallows over a bonfire at Karen's house. But this morning they were going to on the next adventure, the one that they had postponed because of the history class project.

Karen walked over to the shelf, retrieved the hourglass, and with great care, placed it in the center of the

The Garden Club

table. The girls joined hands, took a deep breath, and turned the hourglass over.

A shimmer, a breeze, and the surroundings came into focus. They found themselves in the middle of a group touring an old building. Mel had a sense of *déjà vu*. After looking around for a few minutes, she realized what it was. This was their school! She pulled Karen and Gert aside and whispered, "Do you recognize this building? Look closely; there's something very familiar about it. Look at the desks."

Karen and Gert paused beside Mel and looked around the room. At exactly the same moment, they saw what Mel had seen. "Oh! This is our school! Those are our desks!" Mel shushed them and gave them a quizzical look. *Why would our school be here?*

Karen got it first. "Remember, there was no destination on the card I pulled from the box? There was only a date. There was no *where* to go; there was only a *when*. We're in our hometown. This is New Holstein in 2090!" They stood still for a moment, stunned by what Karen had just said. Could this *really* be New Holstein? Was that even possible?

The girls returned their attention to Sherry, the young woman who was leading the tour. She was in mid-sentence. "…exactly what they are or what they were used for, but it is most likely a religious object. It was found on this altar. It was in a container along with many other items that we have yet to identify." Gert snorted, then quickly coughed to cover the deri-

Chapter 8 - New Holstein, 2090

sive sound. Mel scowled at her, and Karen elbowed Gert and shook her head. Karen asked if it would be okay if they looked around on their own. Sherry nodded and said, "But please don't touch anything. We're still cataloging these pieces."

The girls nodded assent and wandered around the room looking at the familiar things spread out on the desks. The text books were the ones that they were using in 1950, in their own now. One desk held a stack of papers. On closer examination, they saw that the papers were written assignments. Looking at them, Gert noticed three misspelled words in the first short paragraph. She looked at Mel and pointed to the mistakes. Mel nodded and pointed out several punctuation errors. "Wow, this guy sure wasn't paying attention in grammar class!"

After the tour was over, and all the people had left, Sherry heard them talking and noticed that they were pointing at the papers. She came over to where they were standing. "Is there a question? I'll answer it if I can, although this is all so new that we don't have a lot of information on it yet."

Gert chuckled and replied, "No we don't have a question; we were just pointing out the number of misspelled words and grammatical errors in the first paragraph of this essay." Sherry looked questioningly at each of the girls and asked, "How do you know that? We haven't been able to decipher any of the writing yet."

The Garden Club

The girls looked at each other for a moment, wondering how to reply. Karen quickly answered, "My great grandmother was a teacher. She lived to be 100, and she insisted that we all learn how to read and write in script. She was afraid that people were going to lose the ability to read and write cursive, so she taught us all how, and I taught my friends here."

Gert gestured to the stack of papers on the desk. "These are all written assignments for an English class, but I don't think this young man was paying attention when the teacher was giving the grammar lessons."

Sherry looked from one girl to the other, then said, "Wait here. I'll be right back." She dashed out of the room. Gert turned to Karen. "Nice recovery. I'm not sure that's how I'd have explained it, but congratulations on the really quick thinking."

Just then Sherry returned, followed by a tall, skinny man. His hair looked as though it hadn't been combed in a week, and his clothes were rumpled, as if they had been slept in. "This is Mr. Thompson. We just call him Mr. T." Sherry introduced the girls.

"What's this preposterous story Sherry has told me? One of you thinks you can read this? Humph! How can that be? No one here can read it; we haven't had time to decipher it yet."

Karen repeated the story she had just related to Sherry. Mr. T. put on some gloves and gave a pair to Karen. He picked up the top sheets of paper, handed

Chapter 8 - New Holstein, 2090

them to her and said, "Read this." She read it out loud, pointing out and verbally correcting the errors as she did so. Mr. T. looked at her, then turned to Mel and Gert and asked if they could both read it as well. Gert replied, "Yes, sir, we can not only read cursive, but all of us can write it too."

After a moment of thought, Mr. T. asked, "Would you all be so kind as to tell me as much as you can about this 'cursive' writing?" Mel answered immediately, "We'd be happy to help you out. We'll tell you as much about it as we can." Mr. T. picked up the stack of papers, and motioning the girls to follow him, turned and headed to the adjoining room. This room was empty, except for the desk that Mr. T. was using, several student desks, and a long table against the back wall. A row of boxes had been placed on top of the table. Several items had been removed and lined up on the table top. "Now, if you would, I'd appreciate it if you would decipher some of these 'essays,' as you called them."

The girls pulled three desks together in a row. Gert sat in the first one, Karen in the third, and they motioned for Mr. T. to take the middle one. "If you'll sit here, we'll both be able to show you things, and if we write, you can see both things side by side." Karen laid a stack of papers on her desk and sat down. It felt surprisingly right to be sitting at this desk, almost like being in class in her own time. Mr. T. nodded and sat between them.

The Garden Club

Gert looked around for Mel. She was nowhere to be seen, but just as they began reading and pointing out mistakes, Mel clumped into the room. She had a framed document in her hand. "I thought this would help," she said, as she showed him a copy of the Declaration of Independence. "It will give you an idea of how cursive and printing have changed over the years."

Mr. T. looked at Mel and asked, "You mean it's changed more than once? I'd have thought the form of writing for a population would stay the same for the whole group." "Well," replied Mel, "there were so many ethnic groups blending their languages together that spellings and the way the people spoke those languages blended and diverged a number of times. Some letters were written differently by different ethnicities." Mr. T. nodded and murmured to himself, *Well that makes sense.*

After they finished reading, while pointing out grammatical errors and misspellings, Mr. T. asked if they could show him how to write in cursive. Karen and Gert both pointed at Mel. "She has the neatest handwriting," they said in unison. Mel and Gert traded places. While Mel showed Mr. T. how to write, the other two, after asking permission, dug through the boxes. They pulled several more items out and set them on the table beside the others. They finished with all of the writing and unloading of boxes and got up to leave.

As the three girls reached the outer door, Mr. T. called after them, "If I'm not being too presumptuous,

Chapter 8 - New Holstein, 2090

could I ask you to return tomorrow to help us identify some of the things you removed from the boxes? If you need accomodations for the night, just talk to Sherry, she'll find something for you. My sincerest thanks for all your help. Sherry, make some arrangements for these three fine young ladies. I think they'll return tomorrow to help some more."

Sherry nodded, and the girls headed out the door. After they left the building, they wandered around, looking for something familiar. They were beginning to wonder if this really *was* their hometown. Other than the schoolhouse, nothing looked the same. Nothing said "small town Wisconsin."

They circled around town and Mel and Karen sat down on a bench in the park near the schoolhouse. Gert stood facing a building that resembled nothing she had ever seen before. She felt a pang of loss, but why? What could she possibly feel sad about? Her father had been gone for ten of her thirteen years, and her mother was always working. There was nothing here, this specific place, even in this "when," that she could identify as something to be happy about. She suddenly realized that there were tears in her eyes. She glanced back over her shoulder to see if Mel or Karen had noticed. They hadn't. Good. She would never live it down if they saw her crying, for heavens sake!

Meanwhile, Karen was sitting on a bench looking out across the park feeling lost, and, unbelievably, she was missing her siblings, aka the twin unit. She wondered where they were in this "when," and what they were doing. Or what their offspring might be doing. What about her? Had she survived, and did she have any offspring in this "when?" She wasn't sure if she really wanted to know, or if she would be even sadder if she found out. Maybe when she returned to her own "when, she would try to get to know the twins better.

Mel, on the other hand, was very comfortable here. She had no siblings to give her a hard time and no one to tease her about her foot. So far, no one had even appeared to notice it. This was probably only the second time in her life that her deformity had not caused her emotional pain. Here, in this "when," she felt almost normal. She wished her siblings could see her and know how she felt. Maybe then they wouldn't tease her all the time. *Yes, I think I like it in this "when."* The only people from her own "when" who never gave her a hard time about her foot were Gert and Karen. They were more like the people from this "when."

The three girls sat or stood quietly, each with their own private thoughts, unaware of the passage of time. Each looked around furtively to see if the others had noticed their ponderings, then simultaneously reached for their backpacks to eat their snacks. Just as they were finishing up, Sherry found them and said she had a car waiting to take them to their accomodations for the night.

"Okay, just let us get this cleaned up and we'll be right with you," Mel replied.

"Oh, don't worry about that, the 'bots will get it."

Chapter 8 - New Holstein, 2090

The girls looked at each other, shrugged, picked up their backpacks, and followed Sherry back to the schoolhouse. As they neared the school, they saw what looked like a short, fat, wingless airplane parked on the street.

"There's your car. I've already told it where to take you. You know to give it directions when you arrive? Mr. T. said that you were from out of town, and I didn't know if you were familiar with this type of car or not, so I gave it the coordinates of your house. When you want to go somewhere, just give it the coordinates, and tell it to proceed. Do you need a map to help you find your way around?"

"Yes, please," Karen and Gert chorused.

They watched carefully as Sherry palmed open the door. "One of you needs to hold your hand over this decal for about ten seconds so that it can register you as the driver. Then just tell it where you want to go and say "proceed." We'll see you tomorrow. Enjoy your stay. 'bye."

Karen walked up to the car, held her hand over the decal, and counted to ten. The door opened, and a voice announced that it was ready to proceed to the programmed destination. The girls piled in, and Karen said "proceed." It did so, and about five minutes later, it stopped in front of a shiny dome-shaped structure. The doors opened and the voice said, "Destination on your right."

The Garden Club

Taken aback by the disembodied voice, they sat stock-still for a moment before stepping out of the car. The doors closed behind them, as the voice added, "Have a nice day." They walked to the structure, wondering what to do next.

"Well, here we are," Mel said, and a door in the dome slid back. Gert gasped and jumped back, bumping into Karen. Mel stood rooted to the spot. Gert regained her composure first and stepped past Mel and into the dome. Karen was the next one through the door. She grabbed Mel's arm as she stepped past her, and they both stumbled inside. After a brief pause, the door whooshed shut.

"Well," said Karen again, mostly to herself, "I guess we're here, wherever 'here' is."

"I think we should explore," Gert suggested. "I'll check down that section." She nodded to her right. "Karen, why don't you go that way, and Mel, you look over there." She pointed to the other rooms as she spoke. They stood still for a moment, not sure if they could, or should, move. Gert gave Karen a slight shove and started toward the first room. Mel moved next, stumping to the room that Gert had indicated. Karen waited a moment longer, wondering if this was all really happening or if she was dreaming?

Mel walked into what she imagined was a bedroom. There were areas on three walls that had sections that looked like they would fold out. She tried to find something that she might push or slide that

Chapter 8 - New Holstein, 2090

might open them. Nothing. Next, she tried to pull them out manually. Nothing happened. Finally, she said, "Beds." That did it. Three beds folded out of the walls. "Well, that was easy." She walked over to one and laid her backpack on it. *I'll take this one,* she said to herself. She turned and limped out of the room. "I found the bedroom," she called out as she went to find the others.

Gert had turned left when they entered the structure. She stepped through a doorway and into what was obviously the living room. But it was like no living room she had ever seen. There were no floor lamps or ceiling lights. The whole ceiling glowed when she stepped through the doorway. She blinked and said, "Wow, it's so bright in here," and the lights dimmed slightly. "Dimmer, please," and they dimmed some more. "That's perfect!" As she looked around the room, she saw only one chair. That wouldn't do. There were three of them, and they would all want to sit in here. "We need seating for at least three people." Out popped another overstuffed chair and a couch, as well as a coffee table and several end tables. "A fireplace would be nice." Presto! There it was—an electric fireplace with a cozy fire burning in it.

She emerged into the hallway and asked, "Where is everybody? I just found the coolest room! You all need to come and see this."

Karen was in the kitchen. She knew that's what it was because there was a table and four chairs in the middle of the floor, but little else, except bare walls.

The Garden Club

"This is obviously a kitchen, but there's nowhere to prepare food." Those must have been the magic words because, before she could say anything else, a panel opened up in the wall. A voice asked, *"What would you like to eat? Please select a menu from the screen, then tap* PREPARE." Karen jumped and looked around to see who had said that. She was sure it was some kind of a joke. Gert or Mel would definitely do something like that.

She turned and headed for the hallway, sure that the two of them would be out there laughing hysterically. But she found her two friends looking as confused and slightly scared as she was. They all started talking at the same time. Each wanted the other two to come and see what they had discovered.

Karen suggested that they enter the kitchen first, as they were standing just outside of it. While they were there, they ordered hamburgers and fries and sat at the table, eating in silence. After their meal, they explored the rest of the house, finally settling down in the living room. They soon decided that it had been a busy day, and it was probably time for bed.

Karen yawned. Then Mel yawned. Gert chuckled and said, "All right, you've made your point. Who's going to be first in the bathroom?" Two hands shot up, and Gert pointed at Mel. "You first, then Karen, then me. Okay?" Mel stood up and stumped down the hall. A few minutes later, she stuck her head into the room and said ,"Okay, Karen it's all yours. Do either of you care which bed I pick?" The shaking of two heads was

Chapter 8 - New Holstein, 2090

the only response she received. "Okay, good night." Again, the two sleepyheads nodded.

The next morning, the girls rose and watched the beds disappear into the walls before they gathered in the kitchen.

"This is just plain weird, isn't it? You tell it what you want, you say 'prepare,' and it gives you your breakfast hot and ready to eat," Gert exclaimed. They took their time eating, gathered up their belongings, and headed outside. They decided to walk around some more. After all, this *was* their hometown. They must be able to find *something* here that was familiar, that hadn't changed.

A number of people were on the streets. They must be on their way to school or work. Mel noticed it first: everyone was wearing what appeared to be hearing aids. She pointed it out to Karen and Gert and asked what they thought. "Could everybody really be deaf?" she asked. "Sherry wasn't wearing any."

Karen replied, "I wouldn't think so. There must be some other reason for the earplugs."

"That's it," said Gert. "They're not deaf; they're just trying to keep out the general everyday noise. But I wonder. Did you notice that not all the earplugs are the same? Some of them are flashing blue lights, and the people seem to be talking to themselves."

The Garden Club

"But how do they communicate with each other if they're wearing earplugs?" Mel asked. "Maybe we should ask Sherry or Mr. T."

"Excuse me," said Karen, but how do we explain to them why we don't know this. We would have to come up with a reason, and that could lead to a long, complicated explanation."

They discussed the subject for a while and decided not to ask about it.

Returning to their car, they gave it the coordinates for the schoolhouse. Sherry was waiting for them outside. When she asked them if they'd had a good night, they all said, yes, it was very nice. The beds were comfortable, and the food was delicious. There was a moment of uncomfortable silence before Sherry waved, "There's Mr. T. Now we can get started."

Sherry led the girls into the schoolhouse. Mr. T. followed behind them. Sherry went to her desk, and the other three walked into the adjacent classroom. They pulled out the three chairs. Gert and Karen sat down on either side of Mr. T. Mel stumped over to the boxes under the window. The first thing she pulled out was an ink bottle and a fountain pen. The next thing was an old quill pen, one that she remembered Mr. Graves showing them in history class.

Karen spoke first. "At the time those documents we looked at yesterday—those essays—were written, this was what they used to write most things, if a pencil

Chapter 8 - New Holstein, 2090

wasn't appropriate. This pen has a reservoir inside this cylinder. See this silver lever here on the side? You pull the lever down. Then you stick the pen point into the ink bottle, raise the lever, and the ink is drawn into the reservoir. We can't actually do this because the ink is dried up, but I think you can figure out how it would work. The ink is drawn into the groove here on the pen. The ink goes into the nib right here and flows onto the paper as you move it across the sheet."

Karen pointed to the various mechanisms on the pen as she spoke. She went on, "Eventually, these pens were not used as much, because someone invented what was known as a ballpoint pen. The ink was thicker and the pens came with a set amount of ink in their reservoirs. The ink flowed down to the ball. As the ball rolled, the ink was spread across the paper."

Mel held up the crow quill. "Writing with a crow quill is even older," she explained. "That's what was used at the time this framed document was written. You just dipped the crow quill into a container of ink. It took quite a lot of skill not to spill the ink or make blotches all over the paper."

"Thank you. This is so interesting, girls. Now I can see how these items worked. You are lucky that your great grandmother lived long enough to teach you, Karen."

Gert picked up the next item. "This is a pencil sharpener," Mr. T. "Mel, will you hold this down so that I can demonstrate it?" Mel reached across the table and held the sharpener in place Gert picked up a pencil and after an explanation, put the pencil into the appropriately-sized hole and turned the handle on the back of the sharpener. She then pulled out a perfectly sharpened pencil and handed it to Mr. T.

"Excellent! But what are the other holes for?"

"They're for pencils of different diameters. Young children couldn't hold a small diameter pencil very well, so they made larger diameter ones for their little hands. Youngsters didn't have the muscle coordination to control the smaller pencils. There were also smaller sharpeners that could be held in the hand and fit easily into a pencil case."

At about this time, Gert looked at her wristwatch. She had lost all sense of time since they had arrived. Mr.T. noticed her looking at the contraption on her wrist and wondered about it. He had seen a picture of something like it, but he'd never understood how it worked.

"Would it be rude of me to ask what that is that you have on your wrist, Gert?"

"Not at all. It's called a wristwatch. It allowed a person to see the time whenever they wanted to. They were wonderful if you were outdoors or someplace where it wasn't possible to have a large clock displayed where everyone could see it.

"Might I have a closer look at it?"

Chapter 8 - New Holstein, 2090

Gert removed the watch from her arm and handed it to him. He studied it closely for a moment, nodded his head, and handed it back to her.

"Were they all circular?" he asked.

Karen answered his question. "The actual device itself could be almost any shape, but the watch face was almost always circular. The numerals are placed in five-minute increments.. The smaller hand indicates hours, and it moves 1/12th of the way around the face every hour. The longer hand indicates minutes, and it moves 1/60th of the way around the clock every minute. There's a spring inside the watch that makes the gears move that turn the hands. See this little knob on the side? When I turn that, it winds the spring, and the watch will run 24 hours.

Now it was Mel's turn. She held up an item she had found in the bottom of one of the boxes. "I think you'll find this interesting, Mr. T." He reached for the item, examined it closely, and shook his head. He had no idea what it could have been used for. "It's a bottle opener—something I didn't expect to find in a box of school-related items."

He gave her a quizzical look and shook his head again. "Please explain, Mel."

"When my grandmother was a little girl, drinks were put into glass bottles and sealed with a round metal cap. The inside of the cap was lined with a circle of cork that was the exact size of the inner circle of the bottle top. The metal circle was placed on the top of the bottle, crimped down around the outer lip of the glass bottle, so the cork fit tightly into the bottle's opening and sealed it.

"This little metal contraption was used to remove the metal lid from the lip. You see that one end of the opener is D-shaped. The base of the D has a wedge-like piece of metal protruding from it. That small wedge was placed under the crimped edge, and then the rounded top was laid on the center of the metal cap. You had only to lift on the back end of the handle to pop the top off.

"If you'll notice, the other end is triangular in shape and bent downwards where it connects to the handle. That end was used to open cans that held liquids by puncturing the tops. It is not something that was usually found in a schoolhouse. Cans were usually used for beer, but they were also used for condensed milk. Maybe that's why there was an opener in this building."

"What's this thing you call condensed milk, Mel?"

I'll explain that another time. Right now, if you don't mind, I think it's time for us to step outside for a bit of fresh air."

Mr. T. nodded and stood. The girls also stood. They grabbed their backpacks and walked to the front door. Just after they stepped outside, they they felt a slight tremor and noticed a shimmer in the air.

Chapter 8 - New Holstein, 2090

They were once again standing in the clubhouse. The last few grains of sand were just falling into the bottom of the hourglass.

"Well, that was interesting," said Gert.

"Yeah, it's going to take me some time to digest all that," sighed Mel. Brightening, she added, "I wonder where we'll go next time—the future? Or the past?"

"But what if the next adventure takes us—right here? I mean, New Holstein, in our now," Karen speculated, giving the three friends a lot to think about as they pedaled home to get ready for the bonfire at Karen's house.

www.ingramcontent.com/pod-product-compliance
Lightning Source LLC
LaVergne TN
LVHW011732060526
838200LV00051B/3155